A Love Ode

A Devotional Study of Psalm 119

Carl E. Creasman, Jr.

Copyright © 2016, Carl E. Creasman, Jr.

All rights reserved.
No part of this book may be used or reproduced in any manner whatsoever without the written permission of the author and the publisher, except for brief excerpts quoted in critical reviews.

Published by:
Carl E. Creasman, Jr.
P.O. Box 217
Winter Park, FL 32790

www.carlcreasman.com

Printed in the United States of America

ISBN #: 978-0-9814638-4-1

Table of Contents

Day 1 – Introduction... 5
Day 2 – Overview: The General Structure................... 7
Day 3 – Overview: Four Divisions............................... 9
Day 4 – Overview: The Major Themes....................... 11
Day 5 – Aelph: vv. 1-8... 14
Day 6 – Beth: vv. 9-16... 16
Day 7 – Gimel: vv. 17-24... 20
Day 8 – Daleth: vv. 25-32.. 23
Day 9 – Hey: vv. 33-40.. 25
Day 10 – Waw: vv. 41-48... 28
Day 11 – Zayin: vv.49-56... 31
Day 12 – Heth: vv 57-64.. 33
Day 13 – Teth: vv. 65-72.. 36
Day 14 – Yodh: vv 73-80.. 39
Day 15 – Kaph: vv. 81-88... 42
Day 16 – Lamedh: vv. 89-96...................................... 46
Day 17 – Mem: vv. 97-104... 50
Day 18 – Nun: vv 105-112... 53
Day 19 – Samekh: vv 113-120................................... 56
Day 20 – Ayin: vv. 121-128.. 59
Day 21 – Pe: vv. 129-136... 63
Day 22 – Tsadhe: vv. 137-144.................................... 66
Day 23 – Qoph: vv. 145-152...................................... 70
Day 24 – Resh: vv. 153-160....................................... 72
Day 25 – Shin: vv. 161-168.. 75
Day 26 – Taw: vv. 169-176.. 78
Day 27 – Conclusion.. 81

Introduction

It's a love poem.

When it's all said and done, Psalm 119 is a long ode of love to God and His word.

I had read Psalm 119 several times, the first when I was a boy of 11 who decided to read the Bible through. I don't remember much of that first time through God's word to his children, but I do remember how long that Psalm was.

Years later I decided to count the various synonyms of how the Psalmist wrote of God's directions. Words like law, precepts, statutes, and commandments are used repeatedly, like a jackhammer driving home the foundation of life. It was clear enough that in this long Psalm the point was God had given clear rules to obey.

In fact, that idea of obedience became my generalized understanding of the psalm, and in my immaturity and lack of study, I didn't move far from that limited view. I would read the psalm through several other times in the 40 years since that first time, but usually at a quick pace. Going fast helped me get through it all much quicker, and since I was usually simply trying to read through the Bible, or a few other times just reading through the entirety of Psalms…then quicker was better.

But I was wrong. Psalm 119 wasn't some long, repetitive list of rules to obey or even a commanding speech of "obey or else." It is a love poem. I found that out when I decided to take a deep dive into the longest chapter of the Bible. Starting in late 2015, I spent several months reading through the psalm. What I found stunned me and captivated me. It was as if I finally cracked open an old gift box that had once belonged to my grandparents. Saved and appreciated, yet never opened, I had simply enjoyed it for its beauty that was easily seen with a cursory glance. Once opened, it was clear that there was much more to be discovered.

I taught through the psalm over the first six months of 2016 for Numinous Church. We took it one section at a time. You can now use this devotional study book in a variety of ways, but I have written it for you to go day by day. Overall there are 27 days worth, starting with this introduction. If you've never been consistent in your Biblical devotional life, make a promise to yourself to read through these 27 days. Each day is short, no more than 4 pages at the max. You can do this. You too can fall deeply in love with God's word and His ways.

So, I invite you to join me as we unpack the depth of this Psalm. Each of its 22 sections contains brilliance, insight and clues of how to live well. You will be called towards God's Word, have no doubt, and in the midst of His way for you to live, you will find those synonyms of His law. But, you will also find a calling to fall in love with God's direction for your life. I pray you hear as I have His call, like a lover whispering sweet words of life, to find in His commands great delight.

Take a few minutes to pray a thankful prayer to God for His Word. Ask Him to make your heart tender so that you may fall in love with His law as the Psalmist has.

Overview: The General Structure

When you take a look at the longest chapter in the Bible with 176 verses, it's a little bit daunting. I mean, it is longer than II John, Jude, Titus, Philemon and III John combined. So, let's get an overview of what we are about to undertake.

For starters realize the Psalm is an acrostic poem based on the Hebrew alphabet. Hebrew contains 22 letters, so there are 22 sections within the Psalm. Each section corresponds to a letter, each following the successive letters much like we would use the English alphabet to go A, B, C and so forth.

But it gets better. The writer then wrote 8 lines per section and started each verse or stanza with the same Hebrew letter. So, imagine writing a poem using the English language. For the first section, every line would have to start with the letter "A." I have no idea what you'd do with the letter X. It is an amazing act of worship to have written the Psalm this way, and becomes yet another piece of evidence to the creativity of God to lead the writer this way.

As there are 22 sections, then the middle of the Psalm is verse 88, the conclusion of the 11th section of the psalm. That verse could possibly be the theme verse of the psalm; it reads "In your unfailing love, spare my life; then I can continue to obey your laws."

God wants us to follow His ways, His laws. The Psalmist is writing this love ode to that very law. Thus, making the declaration of a desire to obey makes sense. And, as we will see later, the writer acknowledges throughout the Psalm that life is in peril, both from our own potential negative actions and the opposition of others. Yet, the One who gives life is God and He, and He alone, determines if we live or die...thus, the plea for life...but not just so I can live as I wish, but so I can obey.

However, I actually think verse 105 is the real theme verse of the Psalm. You know it well. It's the most famous of the verses: Your word is a lamp to guide my feet and a light for my path. Maybe the King James will trigger it better for you: "Thy word is a lamp unto my feet, and a light unto my path." However you know it, the concept is clearly tied to the thrust of the Psalm. God's law, His precepts will direct you in how to live.

You WANT to know God's word, His ways. Fall in love with it. Cherish it like gold. Study it. Meditate on it. Keep it in your heart. Do this and your path forward in life will be clear. No...it won't tell you what city to live in or which car to purchase, but His underlying principles will provide you direction in any situation, in all cases.

We will come back to verse 105 soon, but for today, write it out. Perhaps email it to yourself. Or, better, go on social media and post it for all the world to see. Put the verse in several places so that you can see it through your day...examples would be in your work area, on the bathroom mirror or in your vehicle.

Overview: Four Divisions

Within the Psalm, as you study, different larger groupings of the 8-verse sections come into view. The first division contains six sections (verses 1-48) and it opens the love poem talking at length about our need to have a passion for God and His law, His ways. Since it is a love poem about God and His ways, it's not surprising that the psalmist starts here. The commands of God are a good for us, so finding that passion to know them is core.

However, others will not appreciate our passion. So, the next division, also six sections (verses 49-96) focus on the fact that opposition will arise against anyone who follows God and His law. This shouldn't be a surprise to anyone, and yet I often get caught off-guard. Things will be sailing along well for me, all the while obeying God's law in many ways of my life…and then some trap will be set for me that will lead me into a spiral. Of course, we know from God's teaching to us through the Apostle Paul, "we fight not against flesh and blood, but against evil rulers and authorities f he unseen world, against mighty powers in this dark world, and against evil spirits in the heavenly places." (Eph 5:12). Or as the Apostle Peter put it, "Stay Alert! Watch out for your great enemy, the devil. He prowls around like a roaring lion seeking for whom to devour." (I Peter 5:8)

The third division (verses 97-136) is perhaps a "catch all" section. Here the Psalmist provides five sections that show what the Word provides. Verse 97 starts us into the first section of this division. Focus on what it says: "Oh, how I love your instructions! I think about them all day long." See it? A love poem about God's way to live. Because they give me life, I think about them all the time….and His ways provide for us.

What does it provide?
> --97-104: wisdom
> --105-112: life guidance
> --113-120: how to live in evil times
> --121-128: what to expect from God, actions desired
> --129-136: obedience

Finally, the last division introduces once again the challenge of living around others who despise or ignore God's way. The psalmist thus turns this collection of the last five sections (verses 136-176) into a focus on our need for rescue. In the midst of being opposed or threatened, we know that only God can rescue us. If you are paying attention, you might notice that I actually started this division with the last verse of the previous section (129-136…part of the third division). I know that verse is part of that section (Hebrew letter Pe/Pey/Pei/Peh), but the cry of the Psalmist really focuses our attention towards the last section. He writes, "Rivers of tears gush from my eyes because people disobey your instructions." Those people who disobey are the ones are putting pressure on God's person to disobey, to forget the law, to turn away from God's ways. We need God to rescue us.

Pray, asking the Holy Spirit to guide you as you read through the Psalm, into which of the four divisions you might need to spend more time.

Overview: The Major Themes

To conclude the overview, there's one more way to come to the Psalm. As you read any part of the Bible, a wonderful way to study it is to see where God uses repeated words or ideas. Those recurrent concepts are a clue to the key ideas of the chapter or Book. As I studied the Psalm over the months, three major concepts or themes became apparent.

Or maybe I should say four concepts or themes. See, of course the law or God's commands is the major theme. It is repeated again and again, multiple times in each section. That was the part I had noted as a child and investigated while in College. It's an important point…as I have noted and will again often, this is a poem focused on what God has said to us.

Three other themes also emerge however after the basic idea of the law of God; first is that there will be opposition to the one who follows that law. Seventeen times through the Psalm, the writer speaks of open opposition. Most of those verses come in that second division, but the idea is really presented throughout the Psalm. Our great enemy does not want us to have a light for our path. Since God's Word is that lamp, then if the enemy can oppose us to the point that we give up…or perhaps better simply quit turning to God's ways…we lose the guidance of light. The verses that speak of the opposition are these: 22, 23, 51, 61, 69, 78, 84, 85, 86, 87, 95, 110, 115, 122, 150, 157, and 161.

That we are opposed should, and does, bring out a reaction from God…and from the Christian. That idea of reaction is the next major theme presented in the Psalm. God will react to those who disregard His law. God also expects His follower to react, and the Psalmist presents that concept connected here. Not surprisingly, many of these verses are closely aligned with the verses of opposition. There are twelve in this category: God reacts (rebukes or acts against): 21, 78, 118, and 119; God's follower reacts: 53, 113, 115, 128, 136, 139, 158, and 163.

The last theme though was the one that surprised me the most. As I have already recounted, I had approached this famous psalm as just a long list of God's laws. That we should obey. That we'd BETTER obey. And, sure, that God's law was good. I knew that; I was living it out as an adult. And yet….

This latter theme presented something that I had not really thought much about. The Psalmist spoke often of his deep desire for God's word. He wrote of having a desire connected with joy at God's ways, God's laws. Honestly, even as I write this, I am still blown away with the passion in the words. This is not the idea of legalism or avoiding punishment. Here is zest. Here is energy. Here is enthusiasm and great enjoyment.

Once when I was in college, I had a girlfriend. I must admit that I was deeply infatuated with her, though I wasn't mature enough to understand that I wasn't anywhere close to the concept of love. In my youthful enthusiasm for her, one day while I was in a long three-hour class, we were given a 15-minute break. This happened long before the days of cell phones, so I had no way to alert her I was coming. Still, I knew she was supposed to be studying at the library, which was about a 10-minute walk away from the building where my class was. I decided that if I ran I could make it quicker, have five minutes with her, and then run back in time for class. So, off I dashed. Sure enough, I found her (she was greatly surprised and happy to see my effort to reach her). We had our moment, and then I dashed back to class. I was a few minutes late, and fortunately for me, was in a class with my favorite professor who liked me and probably gave me more slack than I deserved.

That is what the Psalmist is writing about. A deep desire and passion for God is expressive, like the feeling between two lovers. This theme is throughout the Psalm nineteen times: 14, 16, 20, 36, 40, 47, 54, 58, 72, 77, 97, 103, 111, 127, 131, 143, 161, 162, and 174.

Oh, one more thought here; six of these references speak specifically about have a greater love for God's word than riches.

- v 14: "I have rejoiced in your laws as much as in riches."
- v 36: "Give me an eagerness for your laws rather than a love for money!"
- v 72: "Your instructions are more valuable to me than millions in gold and silver."
- v 111: "Your laws are my treasure; they are my heart's delight."
- v 127: "Truly, I love your commands more than gold, even the finest gold."
- v 162: "I rejoice in Your word like one who discovers a great treasure

What about you? Is your desire for God's word and ways as great as for riches? It's a tough question, but one we must confront. Take time think about something (not a person) that you love deeply. Put it in your mind—could be a favorite childhood possession, perhaps it is fame, maybe it's having people seek your opinion or maybe it is money, wealth. Now…with the thing in your mind, ask for God to awaken in you the same passion as the Psalmist for the commands of God.

Pray, asking God to give you this same eagerness for His laws, great than money, more that gold.

א Aleph (Alef)

1 Joyful are people of integrity, who follow the instructions of the LORD.

2 Joyful are those who obey his laws and search for him with all their hearts.

3 They do not compromise with evil, and they walk only in his paths.

4 You have charged us to keep your commandments carefully.

5 Oh, that my actions would consistently reflect your decrees!

6 Then I will not be ashamed when I compare my life with your commands.

7 As I learn your righteous regulations, I will thank you by living as I should!

8 I will obey your decrees. Please don't give up on me!

The totality of the psalm opens in a place that shouldn't surprise us. The Psalmist's very first suggestion to us is what it means to be a people of integrity. Six things are listed about such a people:

--they are joyful (see also Phil 4:4)
--they follow the instructions of the Lord (see also Prov 13:6)
--they obey His law (see also John 14: 15, 21, 23-24)
--they search for Him with all their heart (see also Heb 11:6)
--they do not compromise with evil (see also Ps 51:4-7 and Prov 6:16-20)
--they walk only in His paths (see also Prov 6:20-23)

Not too surprisingly, this sounds familiar if you remember the very first Psalm in the Bible. Look at vv 1-3

Blessed is the one who does not walk in step with the wicked or stand in the way that sinners take or sit in the company of mockers, but whose delight is in the law of the LORD, and who meditates on his law day and night. That person is like a tree planted by streams of water, which yields its fruit in season and whose leaf does not wither— whatever they do prospers.

Psalm 119:3: *They do not compromise with evil, and they walk only in his paths.* In Psalm 1:1, we are giving more depth to the idea of not compromising with evil. There, passion for God's way is brought in verse 2…"whose delight in the law of the Lord." Both though are showing how God's ways provide a foundation for us to be people of integrity.

Then, 119:4-7 restates what Psalm 1:2 said, that we need God's help to actually walk on this narrow road. The wisdom then to ask for God's help falls into four parts:

--awareness of the demands of God (verse 4)
--need for "my actions" to match God's decrees (verse 5)
--know there will be a judgment, a comparison, both now in this life and later in heaven between my actions and the commands (verse 6); (see also I Peter 2:12, Heb 9:27. I Pet 4:17, II Cor 5:10)
--seeking greater learning, to be a student of God's righteous regulations (verse 7a)

To conclude, look at verse 8…it's a plea and a prayer. Please God don't give up on me. AS I SEEK TO OBEY. Meaning, I am going to try and obey. I have set my focus on His word to do as He commands. But….I know I will slip and fall. So….

Pray with the Psalmist: God, please don't give up on me.

ב Beth (Bet) (Beit)

9 How can a young person stay pure? By obeying your word.

10 I have tried hard to find you— don't let me wander from your commands.

11 I have hidden your word in my heart, that I might not sin against you.

12 I praise you, O LORD ; teach me your decrees.

13 I have recited aloud all the regulations you have given us.

14 I have rejoiced in your laws as much as in riches.

15 I will study your commandments and reflect on your ways.

16 I will delight in your decrees and not forget your word.

The second section of Psalm 119, Beth, provides a road map for how the human can stay pure, especially the young person.

It's a simple answer: Obeying God's Word.

Of course that is not a unique answer to this one psalm. Check out Psalm 111:10 or Proverbs 1:7. The law (or maybe better to say it this way--God's ways) is tied to the "fear of the Lord." The name of our church is Numinous. This is a word I first read from C.S. Lewis in *The Abolition of Man*. I much later came to find out that he had received this idea from a German theologian who was important in his conversion, Rudolf Otto. In his book from the early 1920s, *The Idea of The Holy*, Otto explains this notion of the supreme holiness of God that is beyond us, supreme yet attractive. It represents God has the Wholly Other beyond our comprehension such as who Isaiah saw, and yet also the Immanuel who comes near in the person of Jesus.

We have taught on and emphasized this concept of God since my wife and I started Numinous Inc as a ministry of God back in 1998. This is where our church spent the fall of 2015, reminding ourselves about the need for this understanding of God, on the Numinous aspect of God.

This idea is important as we approach a concept like "obey God's word." If we hear "obey the law" and all we have is religion, then ultimately we'll either feel bad when we fail to perfectly follow, or feel weighed down with "more religious things to do" such as what the Pharisees demanded of the people in Jesus time. Worse, for some, they will turn their own human determination to follow the rules into a Pharisaical demand placed on others.

Remember, Jesus does NOT want us to do that...make human burdens from religious rules. He DOES want us to follow His law. Check out Matt 11:29: "Take my yoke upon you. Let me teach you, because I am humble and gentle at heart, and you will find rest for your souls." Tired of carrying religious burdens? Get rid of them, but take His Yoke. The point he is making is to tied to a firm standard.

How do I do that without feeling the onerous rules? We focus on the Numinous of God, His otherness, His Wholly Otherness that evokes the awe of God, the same feeling as Isaiah did. I realize in His presence that I am unworthy, I should probably be killed...and yet, GLORY, He invites me in to Him. He gives me a path to holiness. Thus, I WANT to draw close to Him. I WANT to be pure. So...back to Psalm 119: 9—How can a young person stay pure...by obeying His word.

How do I pull that off? The Psalmist elaborates:
- Try hard to find God; seek after Him—v. 10 (see also Lk 15:8-10)
- Hide God's word in my heart—v. 11
- Take time to praise God—v. 12
- Recite His word aloud during the day—v. 13
- Rejoice in His law as much as richest—v.14
- Study His commands—v.15a
- Reflect on His ways—v. 15b
- Delight in His decrees—v. 16a
- Remember His word—v. 16b

The concept in verse 14 is the first example of that major theme of a deep desire and passion for God. Verse 16 restates it, but 14 is the powerful thrust of the theme. It is sobering. Think about it.

Every Christian I know would claim to love God. Me too. But, do you, do I, rejoice in His law as I do/would in riches? If I/you won that $1.3 billion lottery from back in 2015....would you rejoice EQUALLY AS MUCH in God's law? More so, the good news is that we already have WON...we HAVE the law, His way for us to live...right here in our hands. Does that fact make you happy? Rejoicing?

 Last thing...verse 16 talks about remembering God's word. "Not forgetting" is both the idea of memorizing AND ALSO remembering the truth of what was said as it impacts your life, your daily. So, for instance, it is good to memorize "For God so loved the world" (John 3:16) but equally important to not forget that in the midst of your day to day, God loves you.

Or, good to memorize "that we know God works all things for the good of those who love God and are the called according to His purpose" (Ro 8:28) BUT EQUALLY important to remember that when things are going weird or hard or seeming persecution, that God is working those things for my good, somehow, even if I can't see it.

Today, write out v. 14. As you did before, place it in multiple locations so that you see it this day, maybe this week. Post it also on social media. Pray for God to bring it up in conversations you have. Just the sheer audacity of it is a great starting point into a discussion about your love for God.

ג Gimel

17 Be good to your servant, that I may live and obey your word.

18 Open my eyes to see the wonderful truths in your instructions.

19 I am only a foreigner in the land. Don't hide your commands from me!

20 I am always overwhelmed with a desire for your regulations.

21 You rebuke the arrogant; those who wander from your commands are cursed.

22 Don't let them scorn and insult me, for I have obeyed your laws.

23 Even princes sit and speak against me, but I will meditate on your decrees.

24 Your laws please me; they give me wise advice.

The third section of the Psalm starts with a plea to God: Be good to me God. Think for a moment about why would you want God to be good to you. What are reasons people generally would give for that desire? When I ask that question of people, I hear things that relate to their own gain, to have safety, maybe to have a good life. If they are Christians, they might give a churchy answer…to have that "life abundant."

The psalmist gives a different answer. He states instead that he wants God to be good to his servant SO THAT I may live and obey. Make sure you notice these are not two separate things--not "may live" and "may obey," but rather "may live and obey."

How does that happen? I need my eyes open to see wonderful truths; I need my eyes open to instruction. Further, I need God to reveal the commands to me. If He hides them, then I won't know what to do.

Verse 20 comes back again to this idea of desire for God...this time he speaks of being overwhelmed. When was the last time you were "overwhelmed with desire"? What was it about? How did you feel?

What do you think it looks like to be "overwhelmed with desire for God's ways"? Don't you think it would feel much the same way? I do. This feeling is something God wants us to start to experience...not just head knowledge about him, but the visceral feeling of emotion as we approach His word.

This is coming back to one of the major themes that His children, His disciples, do not see His commands as something onerous, something to be endured or even something that "I just have to do." Instead, there is a joy....even MORE than a joy, but "overwhelmed with a desire" for God's regulations, His ways.

Verse 21 loops back to where he started...the choice of living and obeying, or not. Here, the Psalmist shows what happens to those who do not "live and obey", who are arrogant and wander from commands. They are cursed by God.

But, even as they oppose the one who follows God ("scorn and insult me"), the focus remains on obeying. Why? Because the law pleases me. God's ways are so good for me that I will meditate on them even as the powerful speak against me.

When facing opposition from others, choose God. To hold a focus on God's law and His ways is right and wise. Note…nothing is said that doing this protects us from opposition.

Pray for same confidence in God as the Psalmist so that when you find opposition you will stay focused on God's ways. Be overwhelmed with a desire for God's regulations, not overwhelmed with fear due to scorn and insults.

ד Daleth (Dalet)

25 *I lie in the dust; revive me by your word.*

26 *I told you my plans, and you answered. Now teach me your decrees.*

27 *Help me understand the meaning of your commandments, and I will meditate on your wonderful deeds.*

28 *I weep with sorrow; encourage me by your word.*

29 *Keep me from lying to myself; give me the privilege of knowing your instructions.*

30 *I have chosen to be faithful; I have determined to live by your regulations.*

31 *I cling to your laws. LORD, don't let me be put to shame!*

32 *I will pursue your commands, for you expand my understanding.*

Have you ever been exhausted? I don't mean simply tired. No, I mean so out of energy that you feel as if one more exertion of effort would perhaps be damaging to yourself. When that time comes, just about all you can do is lie down. Exhausted. Out of gas.

Sometimes though, the exhaustion isn't so much physical as it is emotional. This is where the Psalmist is in the third section, Daleth. You see that in the first lines… "I lie in the dust." Unable to move. Overwhelmed.

But not forever, thankfully, because God hears us. He comes to our rescue. So, I share my ideas and plans with God and He listens. We know of course that God has said elsewhere that it is unwise for humans to think too highly of their own plans (Prov 16:9, James 4:13-15). However, He isn't mocking His servant, the disciple who in communion with God shares her thoughts.

So, I share my ideas with God and He listens. Then my job is to sit to be taught. Note, this teaching is not about the validity or issues with my plans, but rather for God to teach me His decrees. I need, then, the understanding of His commandments (v. 27, 32) so that I will not lie to myself (v. 29) and to avoid being put to shame (v.31).

Note one more thing. In verse 28, there is a tender honest moment by the writer. "I weep with sorrow; encourage me by Your word." I've been there. In fact, I would offer that my last five years have felt this way…emotionally weary to the point that I often weep with sorrow. I need God's encouragement.

The Psalmist my be simply responding to the feeling that life itself has grown difficult or maybe overwhelming due to persecution. Either way, the sentiment is a sad, weary point that echoes the first verse of the section. I "lie in the dust" needing to be "revived" as I "weep with sorrow," I so desperately need God's encouragement.

God longs to do that for you. How? The encouragement comes "by Your word." See…it's a love poem. In the midst of my weariness to the point that I lay down, perhaps lay down to simply waste away, God brings encouragement through His word.

Are you weary? Heavy of heart? Realize that the encouragement God wants to bring you lies in the Bible itself. Open it and read. Maybe read these first 32 verses of Psalm 119 again. Perhaps turn to something Jesus said such as in Matthew 11 or John 13-17. Psalm 23 always encourages me to know that as my Good Shepherd, He walks with me protecting, feeding, and guiding.

ה Hey (He) (Hei)

33 Teach me your decrees, O LORD; I will keep them to the end.

34 Give me understanding and I will obey your instructions; I will put them into practice with all my heart.

35 Make me walk along the path of your commands, for that is where my happiness is found.

36 Give me an eagerness for your laws rather than a love for money!

37 Turn my eyes from worthless things, and give me life through your word.

38 Reassure me of your promise, made to those who fear you.

39 Help me abandon my shameful ways; for your regulations are good.

40 I long to obey your commandments! Renew my life with your goodness.

In this section, the Psalmist gives God orders. It's direct. It's clear. The Psalmist wants to be faithful to God and he knows that unless God does it, there is little hope that it will happen. Look at the list of commands

- Teach me your decrees (v. 33)
- Give me understanding (v 34)
- Make me walk along the path of your commands (v 35)
- Give me an eagerness for your laws (v. 36)
- Turn my eyes from worthless things (v. 37a)
- Give me life (v. 37b)
- Reassure me of your promise (v. 38)
- Help me abandon my shameful ways (v. 39)
- Renew my life (v. 40b)

As I said, the writer wants this long list of requests met for one reason…and he says it openly in v. 49: "I long to obey your commandments!"

He restates four times that this obedience is a best thing. In v34b, he states that he will put the instructions into practice "with all my heart." Verse 35b explains that walking on the path of God's way is "where my happiness is found." Down towards the end of the section in verse 39, he writes "your regulations are good."

However, his strongest statement comes in verse 36. *Give me an eagerness for your laws rather than a love for money!* Remember hearing this earlier? Exactly…back in verse 14 of the second section (Beth). There it was to "rejoice in laws AS MUCH as riches." This time the focus is "**rather than** a love of money."

Paul, writing to his disciple Timothy made this same point. In I Timothy 6:6-10 Paul perhaps is even thinking of these verses from Psalm 119. He first reminds Timothy "godliness with contentment is great gain. Yet, the warning is that a deep wanting for riches is a "Temptation and a trap." Finally, in verse 10, Paul writes, "For the love of money is a root of all kinds of evil. Some people, eager for money, have wandered from the faith and pierced themselves with many griefs." See it…love of money is the root of all kinds of evil, and evidence of this fact is seen that many have wandered away from the faith, or as the Psalmist would note, from God's laws.

For myself, I have to battle this pull towards riches. I have found the best way for me is to move towards a simple life, towards the giving away of things and money to the poor, to those in need. Even if you are someone who feels as if you don't have many things or much money, sharing your resources are a way to break the potential of that lure of money.

So, read again the Psalmist's words: Give me an eagerness for your laws.... One of God's laws is to care for the least, the widow, the orphan, for the other person who has needs. When we taught this section at our worship service, we didn't spend time singing or even hearing much speaking. Instead, we put God's command to care for the poor, for the lonely, for the broken into practice. We made "blessing bags" to keep in our cars, ready to be given to anyone in need of food. The bags include various food items that are non-perishable including soup in a box, tuna packs, beef jerky, fruit cups, pudding, water and few other items, all put into a gallon clear ziplock-style bag.

God warns us not to have a love or desire for wealth. Instead have a love or desire, an eagerness for God's laws.

This week, put together your own "blessing bag" to keep in the car. You can purchase items on sale at your grocery store or larger warehouse store. Even if you feel like you have limited resources, you can put together a simple bag like this…or, if that seems to take too much time, go buy a few $5 gift cards to Subway or Chick-fil-a (a healthy fast-food option). Then, next time you see someone with a little cardboard sign asking for help, give them the gift card or the blessing bag. Choose intentional acts, practices, to help strengthen your own resolve to not have a love of money, but rather a love for God's law.

ו Waw (Vav)

41 LORD, give me your unfailing love, the salvation that you promised me.

42 Then I can answer those who taunt me, for I trust in your word.

43 Do not snatch your word of truth from me, for your regulations are my only hope.

44 I will keep on obeying your instructions forever and ever.

45 I will walk in freedom, for I have devoted myself to your commandments.

46 I will speak to kings about your laws, and I will not be ashamed.

47 How I delight in your commands! How I love them!

48 I honor and love your commands. I meditate on your decrees.

Think about movies that you've seen. See if you can remember a movie moment when the idea of "being honored, getting approval, being complimented" is shown in the movie or story. Got one?

One of my favorite moves is *Saving Private Ryan*. In what may be the best moment of the film, the Captain, played by Tom Hanks, is perplexed by what his next step should be. So, in some despair, he turns to his faithful Sergeant to ask his opinion. Their conversation turns the movie towards its dramatic conclusion.

Another excellent film is *Mister Holland's Opus*. Here, at the end of the movie as the titular protagonist believes that his life has been wasted, he is surprised by a gathering in the school auditorium. He is honored by 100s of former students and their families to show him how much he meant to them and impacted their lives.

Or, for a more recent example, in the Pixar movie *Inside Out*, the little girl, inside whose head the embodied emotions have been interacting, is saved when the lead emotion, Joy, realizes that she needs to allow Sadness to "drive" the brain/emotions. As she honors her friend with control, the story changes for the better.

How about your personal life? Can you think of a time when you were honored at work or school, with an award or a nice compliment?

Turn in your Bible to look at I Corinthians 13, the famous "love" chapter. Here we read that love is described as "not rude…keeps no record of being wronged…does not rejoice in injustice…." On the one side is love, in which honor is connected, and on the other side is taunting. That word can be understood as to mock, jeer, goad, insult, tease, or deride.

The Psalmists presents this pairing…that I get taunted because I trust in God's word…and thus I will honor and love God's commands

With the knowledge of God's laws…
    …I can answer those who question my faith, who taunt me (v.42)
    …I will walk in freedom (v.45)
    …I will be able to speak boldly, even to those in power (v. 46a)
    …I will not be ashamed (by my words, actions, defense) (v.46b)

So, to secure this knowledge (what must I do)
   --I will obey forever…so put Your laws into action (v. 44)
   --I will devote myself…cherish the laws, make them central in my life (v 45b)
   --I will delight in Your commands…enjoy, move toward them with pleasure (47)
   --I will honor and love…hold the laws in highest regard (v. 48)
   --I will meditate…think slowly, deeply, repeatedly (v. 49)

Note that first God gives unfailing love and salvation. (v. 41) So I am not having to do these things in the hope that He will do something in return, but rather in RESPONSE to His first action of love to me.

Lastly, walk in confidence because He does NOT ever snatch away the Word of Truth. In Romans 8:35-39, Paul gives us this wonderful promise again. So, we live a life in pursuit of holiness.

Focus your prayer on the five actions to secure the knowledge of God's laws. Pick one to meditate on and put into action this day.

ז Zayin

49 Remember your promise to me; it is my only hope.

50 Your promise revives me; it comforts me in all my troubles.

51 The proud hold me in utter contempt, but I do not turn away from your instructions.

52 I meditate on your age-old regulations; O LORD, they comfort me.

53 I become furious with the wicked, because they reject your instructions.

54 Your decrees have been the theme of my songs wherever I have lived.

55 I reflect at night on who you are, O LORD; therefore, I obey your instructions.

56 This is how I spend my life: obeying your commandments.

With this section, we now move into the second larger division of the psalm (vv. 49-96). Here, as we explained in the overview, the focus shifts to the concept of opposition, and how there are those who hate anyone who follows God. Worse, rather than simply not liking us, or the actions of the one who loves God, these are shown as taking specific actions to oppose, trap, taunt or trip up the believer.

This idea of finding opposition is also one of our three major themes. Here are those verses again: 22, 23, 51, 61, 69, 78, 84, 85,

86, 87, 95, 110, 115, 122, 150, 157, and 161. As you can see, a large bulk of these verses come in this second division of the psalm.

For this day, re-read the verses above for the section. Go slowly. Take your time. Write down at least three observations or notes from the section. You can do it. See if one of the verses really speaks to you.

The Psalmist starts by claiming the God's promise is the only hope. It's as if he knows more opposition is soon to come. But the promise does more…it also revives the one who walks with God. Thirdly, God's promise comforts me. Why do I need comfort? Well, as is written, because of the troubles that come my way.

What troubles, you may wonder? The Psalmist shares it…there are proud people holding him in contempt (v. 51). Have you been there before? I have. You feel as if you are simply trying to live like a Christian, and suddenly you realize that you are the target of attack, of harsh words. In the midst of that, God's comfort comes as I meditate on His word.   So, while the wicked person refuses God's instruction, what we find is that same set of instructions is a comfort.

My life—both the ordering of my steps and my last thoughts at night—is based on God's instructions and commands.

On the day that we did our own Bible study in worship, I urged everyone to write down one specific verse that God highlighted. For me, it was v. 54: *Your decrees have been the theme of my songs wherever I have lived.* Perhaps that one speaks to me because I have written many worship songs, and since I love to write songs, I hoped that His word was also "the theme of my songs."

As we have done two previous times, write out the one verse that really spoke to you from this section. Place copies of it around where you can see it this day. Then, take to social media and share it with others. Tell them why you are posting the verse and then ask the Holy Spirit to open other conversations where you can share your verse.

ח Heth (Chet) (Cheit)

57 LORD, you are mine! I promise to obey your words!

58 With all my heart I want your blessings. Be merciful as you promised.

59 I pondered the direction of my life, and I turned to follow your laws.

60 I will hurry, without delay, to obey your commands.

61 Evil people try to drag me into sin, but I am firmly anchored to your instructions.

62 I rise at midnight to thank you for your just regulations.

63 I am a friend to anyone who fears you— anyone who obeys your commandments.

64 O LORD, your unfailing love fills the earth; teach me your decrees.

In this second section in the second division on Opposition, the Psalmist starts with a clear declaration of faith. Lord, You are mine! He then follows it up with a promise. Not surprisingly, its connected to obedience with the ways of God that are bringing the opposition.

But then the section also deals with directions for life. How do I find my path to walk forward.

He starts with the promise. Obedience is not merely something that emerges from your mouth; some sort of words only. The brother of Jesus speaks of this very thing. James, writing to the church in Jerusalem, tells them clearly that obedience comes in actions:

> What good is it, my brothers and sisters, if someone claims to have faith but has no deeds? Can such faith save them? Suppose a brother or a sister is without clothes and daily food. If one of you says to them, "Go in peace; keep warm and well fed," but does nothing about their physical needs, what good is it? In the same way, faith by itself, if it is not accompanied by action, is dead. But someone will say, "You have faith; I have deeds." Show me your faith without deeds, and I will show you my faith by my deeds.

So the Psalmist makes the open declaration to obey. But then what?

--ponder direction to go (v. 59a)
--turn to follow your laws (v. 59b)
--Hurry to obey (v. 60)
--Firmly anchored in God's ways even as evil tries to drag me another way...into sin.
--rise at midnight, to thank God for just regulations

Thus, I need to be aware of Who guides, and in guiding, protects. God. God alone. That He guides me is why I come back, I return to His ways.

Lastly, note that following God's starts first in mind, with my spirit's desire to walk His ways. Meaning, I commit to God's ways

BEFORE getting any actual steps or direction from God. One of my favorite passages about following God comes from Proverbs 3:5-6.

> Trust in the LORD with all your heart and lean not on your own understanding; in all your ways submit to him, and he will make your paths straight.

I have to be willing to trust God first. Then, I have to decide to not trust or lean on human understanding. And finally, in all my ways submit to HIS WAYS. Only then is God "on the hook" to guide you. He will do it. He will "make your path straight," but the first action is ours.

Determine this day to put your mind in the same place as the Psalmist, that after pondering the direction of your life, you turn to follow His ways. Pray now, and tell God that this day, you are determined to hurry without any delay to follow his commands.

ט Teth (Tet) (Teit)

65 *You have done many good things for me, LORD, just as you promised.*

66 *I believe in your commands; now teach me good judgment and knowledge.*

67 *I used to wander off until you disciplined me; but now I closely follow your word.*

68 *You are good and do only good; teach me your decrees.*

69 *Arrogant people smear me with lies, but in truth I obey your commandments with all my heart.*

70 *Their hearts are dull and stupid, but I delight in your instructions.*

71 *My suffering was good for me, for it taught me to pay attention to your decrees.*

72 *Your instructions are more valuable to me than millions in gold and silver.*

Think about your education journey. Can you remember a favorite teacher that inspired you? Someone you remember for how they impacted your life? If you are like me, you probably have more than one. What was it about that person that really has captured your memory?

I think of Mrs. Gamble who taught me in the Seventh and Eighth grade. She was also both loving and strict. I wanted to please her, yet kept her in an awe. In High School, Mrs. Fogarty was my history teacher. She was quite brilliant, deeply knowledgeable of the information presented, yet she was also fun to be with. In College, Professors Dr. Bond, Dr. Bohanon, and Dr. Rea all inspired me in different ways, yet so memorably. Dr. Bond was a faithful guide through my entire Master's Degree program. Dr. Bohanon started at Auburn at the same time as I was there as a freshman; she was young and witty, yet clearly a superior intellect. Dr. Rea was the advisor for the Master's degree students and was quite scary. Yet, as I took him for two different English History classes, I was inspired to reach for academic heights that previously I had never considered.

Obviously, teaching is the theme of this section of the Psalm. As you think about teachers that impacted you, there is no better teacher than God Himself. The Psalmist requests that God be the teacher. There is a clear recognition of the value of God teaching through His word:

--provides good judgment, knowledge—v. 66
--takes discipline from the Teacher—v. 67
--discipline keeps me from wandering—v. 67
--discipline and the teaching is good for me—v. 68
--even as my reputation is lied about, smeared…the truth shows up in my actions, and that fact demonstrates that I obey the commandments with all of my heart—v. 69
--find delight in instructions—v 70 (the person who does not delight in instruction?? Their hearts are "dull and stupid.")
--the discipline and/or the teaching, which can feel like suffering, is good—v. 71
--the teaching of His instructions is worth more than gold and silver.—v. 72 (note that this is the third time uses reference of money to make the point…previously vv. 14 and 36)

So this focus on teaching touches on my need for a God-like perspective:

--what feels like suffering can actually be part of discipline or teaching, and thus is good for me
--the attack from arrogant people are really smears and lies; there is a truth about me that in fact I am obeying God's commands. So, my suffering is not because of some sin of mine. Peter teaches this same thing years later, writing in I Peter 4:14-16 that if you suffer it must not be for [major sins] like murder, stealing or even prying. This notion of Peter is reflected here in the Psalm that what protects me is my obedience to God's commands…obedience with all my heart.
--wander…discipline…follow---when hard things are happening in your life, one question you should ask is "have I wandered from God's instructions"?

Pray to the Father God, King of the Universe, asking Him to help you to patiently sit at His feet as a student, eager to learn His lessons of how to live.

׳ Yodh (Yod)

73 *You made me; you created me. Now give me the sense to follow your commands.*

74 *May all who fear you find in me a cause for joy, for I have put my hope in your word.*

75 *I know, O LORD, that your regulations are fair; you disciplined me because I needed it.*

76 *Now let your unfailing love comfort me, just as you promised me, your servant.*

77 *Surround me with your tender mercies so I may live, for your instructions are my delight.*

78 *Bring disgrace upon the arrogant people who lied about me; meanwhile, I will concentrate on your commandments.*

79 *Let me be united with all who fear you, with those who know your laws.*

80 *May I be blameless in keeping your decrees; then I will never be ashamed.*

The psalm now presents two groups of people with whom we interact in throughout our lives:

--those who fear (awe, reverence) God—vv 74,79
--arrogant people who lie—v 78, see also v. 69

I have a choice to make, confronted with this reality...follow God or not. I choose to follow God, thus I belong to the first group...those who fear God. This is good for me, but also wonderful for others around me. My choice to follow God's commands becomes an encouragement to others; those other people who ALSO want to follow God's commands thus "find in me a cause for joy for I have put my hope in Your word."

God's concept for being "of His people" is that the disciple's journey is not a solo operation. Throughout the Bible, both Old and New Testaments, we see God speaking about the plural. "My people," "Those who are called by My name," "My disciples," "the people of God," "the body of Christ," "the army of God." Even the word we have translated as "church" really means ONLY a plural existence: the called out ones. Plural.

Think of it this way. The individual who believes and follows God is known as the disciple or, after Acts, the Christian (the little Christ). Yet, when Jesus says that "when two or three are gathered in My name, I am there" he is now speaking of the "called out ones" or "the church." One person who believes in God is a Christian. Two or more people who believe in God are church. Here, in Psalms, we see a key concept of this togetherness in that we are to encourage each other.

As I look around at my fellow believers, when I see them following God's commands, putting their hope in God's word, then I find my own cause for joy! I see them choosing the narrow way, and though I may feel discouraged, weak or tired, I now am encouraged by their faith. This is why at the end of the section, in verse 79, we see that our unity is vital to life, hinting at even a level of protection.

Equally important, my choice to follow God's commands also brings me protection and comfort. In verses 76-77, the Psalmist cries out for God's comfort, a promise God has made and for Him to "surround me with your tender mercies so I may live." This is why we see yet again that there is love, delight, even joy, for God's instructions (v. 77b). The Psalmist is overwhelmed with delight knowing that God is there as a comfort and a surrounding wall of mercy.

Your choice to follow God's ways will cause a reaction from the second group of people, those who arrogantly reject God's ways. So, in the midst of life, there will often be attack from the arrogant people who lie about you. Whether it is from jealousy or anger, perhaps a misguided discontent with how they perceive Christians in the world, the choice to be devoted to God and His ways will not be popular. These people will lie about me and my actions.

What should we do with that?
- "I will concentrate on Your commands."
- I will "be united with all who fear You."
- May I be "blameless in keeping Your decrees."

And what, then, is the end result as I keep his decrees? "I will never be ashamed."

Pray, asking the Father, as I go through life today, help me to keep my focus on You and Your word, and not on others who may attack me verbally or lie about me. You alone are judge. Help me to be an instrument of your peace to others, and keep my focus on keeping Your commands and being united with others. Help me to see the faithful walk of other Christians who follow Your commands that I may see their lives as a cause for joy...and then help me to equally be a cause for joy in their life.

‫כ‬ Kaph (Kaf)

81 *I am worn out waiting for your rescue, but I have put my hope in your word.*
82 *My eyes are straining to see your promises come true. When will you comfort me?*
83 *I am shriveled like a wineskin in the smoke, but I have not forgotten to obey your decrees.*
84 *How long must I wait? When will you punish those who persecute me?*
85 *These arrogant people who hate your instructions have dug deep pits to trap me.*
86 *All your commands are trustworthy. Protect me from those who hunt me down without cause.*
87 *They almost finished me off, but I refused to abandon your commandments.*
88 *In your unfailing love, spare my life; then I can continue to obey your laws.*

With our arrival at Kaph, we have come to the middle of the psalm. This is section 11, out of the 22 in total. Verse 88 is the middle verse of the entire psalm, and in some senses could be seen as a theme of the division about opposition. We want God to spare our lives. This section also comes towards the tail end of the opposition division; the Psalmist has now built to a crescendo the feeling and frustration of being opposed simply for loving God's ways. This section has the most verses from the theme about the opposition: 84, 85, 86, and 87.

That there is so much focus on the strength of the opposition thus helps explain why this section presents the one who follows God's ways at the weakest, at the most tired. This section more than any other is a sad, pleading lament for God to bring aid. I am fully spent.

Look at the way this feeling is expressed:

- 81a—worn out waiting on rescue
- 82a—straining my eyes hoping to see rescue (rescue="promises come true")
- 82b—need comfort from being attacked
- 83—I am shriveled
- 84a—waiting, waiting, waiting for rescue, for God to punish those who persecute
- 85—arrogant people, sly people who dig traps,---why "hate Your instructions"
- 86b-87a—hunters come to finish me off (to kill me)

Have you felt that in your life? Many have…a sense of being hunted, of being attacked to the point that we feel shriveled, worn out. You perhaps have never been physically lost, but surely you've seen some movies that show this idea of being in great need of rescue, and then looking to the horizon in hopes of seeing a hint of help coming.

One of the great challenges of being a Christian is trying to reconcile what Jesus says when He declares that He has come to give us life, and life abundant. For many, the idea of a better life, of life abundant, sounds very much like life with no or limited pain or struggle.

However, Jesus also clearly says that those who follow Him will walk on a difficult narrow way. That such a person will find themselves facing opposition even from family. And that in the end, the idea of following him is, as German theologian Dietrich Bonheoffer said, a call to come and die. Well, wait a minute…how is a call to come and die on a narrow, difficult road of life the same as life abundant?

Ultimately, that idea would take far more space than this devotional guide, but surely we must consider that how God defines "life abundant" is different from ours. And Jesus, along with his main disciple writers in the New Testament, gives many descriptions of how the journey of the Christian will be a hard one…hard in the sense of not comfortable, not without pain, not without loss, and not without struggles. So, if anyone needs to look to the horizon for aid, it is the disciple.

We know that it is not by our own strength that we make it through. We are not called to just "tough it out" or "suck it up." Rather, we are told more clearly that God's strength is made perfect, or seen more clearly, in our weakness. And, that God works through our weakness, through our struggles, in order to project His own glory.

So, in the midst of that persecution, what is the action of God's child? To still stay focused on God's ways:

- 81b—put my hope in your word
- 83—not forgotten to obey your decrees
- 86a—your commands are trustworthy
- 87b—I refuse to abandon your commandments

As stated, v. 88 summarizes this section, and perhaps the entire division. In verse 87, the Psalmist acknowledges that he is almost dead. And yet, instead of giving up or giving in, the one who follows God REFUSES to abandon God's commandments. Thus, *In your unfailing love, spare my life; then I can continue to obey your laws.* The plea to God goes up to spare my life. Why? So that I may remain alive? No. So that I may avoid pain or persecution? No.

So that I can continue to obey God's laws.

Remember…it's a love poem. God's ways are my desire, more than a desire for riches. As you find yourself in whatever trouble around you, whether personal or national, this verse shows how the Christian should stand.

Not looking for retribution. Not assuming escape from pain or attack. Rather, in a consistent pursuit, willingly, of God's ways.

Pray to God, asking.... come to my aid. Spare my life. Give me strength for another day, and as I take that next breath, walk that next step, like my words and actions show that I will continue to obey your laws and your ways!

ל Lamedh (Lamed)

89 Your eternal word, O LORD, stands firm in heaven.

90 Your faithfulness extends to every generation, as enduring as the earth you created.

91 Your regulations remain true to this day, for everything serves your plans.

92 If your instructions hadn't sustained me with joy, I would have died in my misery.

93 I will never forget your commandments, for by them you give me life.

94 I am yours; rescue me! For I have worked hard at obeying your commandments.

95 Though the wicked hide along the way to kill me, I will quietly keep my mind on your laws.

96 Even perfection has its limits, but your commands have no limit.

The previous five sections have mentioned often that life for the one who follows God can be difficult as you find yourself opposed. It's a great challenge, and in the midst of that, the Devil's most often attack is to suggest that you are suffering for nothing. He might try to convince you that there is no God, or maybe worse that God isn't concerned with your issues. He will suggest that

God will not come to help you. So, it isn't surprising that the Psalmist wants to answer that charge from the enemy.

Verses 89-91 reminds that in the midst of all the opposition, God's word is secure forever. God and His word is:
- firm in heaven
- extends to all generations
- endures as the earth
- true to this day

Perhaps this attack is why God, speaking through Paul, urges us to have a helmet on during the battle of life. And what is the helmet…that of the promise of salvation. Paul explains this both to the church at Ephesus and to the one in Thessalonica. To the Thessalonians, he is specific that the point is the "hope of salvation." Our enemy wants us to think that maybe God will not come through for us…but we hold to hope in God, and to His promise to bring us home safely.

Why does it matter? For all things that happen serve God's plans. This is a vital thing to consider. Not to trail off into the 2000 year old debate between predestination and free will, but it is clear that God has His own plans for the world. And we know those plans are designed to magnify His glory through the world, the ultimate good for the world. So, in one sense, life attacks we face still demand our holding to the hope of salvation because we can know with confidence that all these things serve His greater plan.

Even better, though, is realizing that the faithfulness of God's word is critical for "my life success" because it will sustain me through misery. Without his faithfulness, "I would have died." So, you can link verse 89 to 92…God's word is eternal, standing firm, and because it is such, I can find joy in it, being sustained by it. Without it, the Psalmists admits he would simply have died in his misery.

So, along the way, which really means as one goes on the journey through life—God's word sustains with joy. Then verses 93-94 restate this fact. I will never forget God's way because it gives me life. I cry out for His rescue, can claim that he SHOULD rescue me because "I work hard at obeying Your commandments."

Even though the wicked (those who oppose God and His ways, and anyone who tries to walk in His ways) hide to kill me along the way, I will keep my mind focused on the law. Never lose sight of the fact that the enemy wants to destroy you. If he can do that by physically killing you, he will. But, if he can destroy you by convincing you to give up on God, to back off on your passion for God or believe that God's word isn't necessarily all that faithful, he will do that too.

So, how does the disciple stay focused in the midst of attack, through all the misery, sadness, disappointment, or opposition of life?

- never forget your commandments (v. 93)
- work hard at obeying your commandments (v. 94)
- keep mind on the law (v. 95)

The disciple does these three things because of the promises given in the first four verses of the section....ultimately that God's word is secure.

In the end, the summary of the section reminds that human action, even perfect action, has limits; God has no limits.

Are you under attack? Have you experienced attack before? Has the enemy suggested to you that God may not actually be as faithful to you as you wish? Are there fears that God isn't concerned or doesn't know about your situation? Re-read vv. 89-91 a few times. Say them as declarations. With exclamation points! God is faithful. Then remind yourself of your tasks (vv. 93-95) in remembering the commandments. If you aren't sure which of His many commandments to keep in mind, just focus and meditate on what Jesus said was the greatest commandment: "'Love the Lord your God with all your heart and with all your soul and with all your mind.' This is the first and greatest commandment. And the second is like it: 'Love your neighbor as yourself.'"

מ Mem

97 Oh, how I love your instructions! I think about them all day long.

98 Your commands make me wiser than my enemies, for they are my constant guide.

99 Yes, I have more insight than my teachers, for I am always thinking of your laws.

100 I am even wiser than my elders, for I have kept your commandments.

101 I have refused to walk on any evil path, so that I may remain obedient to your word.

102 I haven't turned away from your regulations, for you have taught me well.

103 How sweet your words taste to me; they are sweeter than honey.

104 Your commandments give me understanding; no wonder I hate every false way of life.

With the Mem section, the Psalmist moves into the third division of Psalm 119. This grouping of five sections provides a look at "what the Word provides." Here, in Mem, we are shown that the Word provides wisdom. Not surprisingly, a review of the book of Proverbs would be in order here.

After opening with yet another call to constantly be thinking about and meditating on God's instructions, the Psalmist states what the Proverb writers explain…God's commands for life make us wise.

Insight for living comes through knowing and obeying God's commands.

If I think about God's instructions, God's commands, all day long, then:

--I will be wiser than enemies
--I will gain a constant guide
--I will have more insight than teachers
--I will become wiser than elders

Take time to read in the first five chapters of Proverbs. The following verses all come back, ultimately, to the same point that the Psalmist is making...God's rules for life with guide you through life with wisdom: 1:3, 1:5, 1:8-9, 1:23, 2:1-3, 2:4-5, 2:6-8, 2:9-11, 2:12, 2:20, 3:1-2, 3:5-6, 3:7-8, 3:13-15, 3:21-23, 4:1-2, 4:5-6, 4:10-11, 4:14-15, 4:18-19, 4:23, 5:1-2, and 5:21-23

Because I think about "your instructions" all day long, then "I refuse to walk on any evil path." Psalm 1 also makes this point. Blessed is the person who doesn't walk, stand or sit with those who refuse to follow God's ways.

This provides a circle for life success (101-102):

--the disciple refused to walk on any evil path in order to remain obedient

--in being obedient, God has "taught me well" meaning, I am given insight and wisdom...and with that knowledge, I know to NOT walk on any evil path.

So God's laws and commands are sweet to my taste. Again, this idea of the desire for God's ways. But they are also sweet to me because the Word teaches me to avoid any evil path. In other words, as I enjoy the sweet tasting Word of God, I then have understanding for life.

Thus, the Psalmist takes us back to the point about the correct path: "no wonder I hate every false way of life." Why do I know to hate every false way---because I have understanding. With my wisdom and insight, I realize that the fear of the Lord is the beginning of wisdom, so I know to keep digging deeply into His ways. So, back to the start of the section…the disciple thinks about God's commands for life all day long!

Pray to the Father to be given more wisdom. Help me, oh God, with that wisdom, to think about your commands all day long.

נ Nun

105 *Your word is a lamp to guide my feet and a light for my path.*

106 *I've promised it once, and I'll promise it again: I will obey your righteous regulations.*

107 *I have suffered much, O LORD ; restore my life again as you promised.*

108 *LORD, accept my offering of praise, and teach me your regulations.*

109 *My life constantly hangs in the balance, but I will not stop obeying your instructions.*

110 *The wicked have set their traps for me, but I will not turn from your commandments.*

111 *Your laws are my treasure; they are my heart's delight.*

112 *I am determined to keep your decrees to the very end.*

With the arrival at verse 105, we come to what I believe is the theme verse of the entire psalm. In this imagery of light on a path, we are given a summation of the overall thrust---a love ode to God's law with the point of having guidance for life. This is probably the most quoted verse of the Psalm, and for obvious reason. Looking for life guidance is one of the most requested topics of discussion among Christians. What should I do with my life? What decision should I make next?

Needing answers to those questions, needing life guidance, is the point of this section, the second one in the "what the Word provides" division. Last section we saw that the Word of God provides wisdom. Now we see that it provides life guidance. Psalm 1, which we referenced before, highlights this same sentiment, the idea of God's guidance.

> Blessed is the one who does not walk in step with the wicked or stand in the way that sinners take or sit in the company of mockers, but whose delight is in the law of the LORD, and who meditates on his law day and night. That person is like a tree planted by streams of water, which yields its fruit in season and whose leaf does not wither— whatever they do prospers.
>
> Not so the wicked! They are like chaff that the wind blows away. Therefore the wicked will not stand in the judgment, nor sinners in the assembly of the righteous. For the LORD watches over the way of the righteous, but the way of the wicked leads to destruction.

Here, in one single verse, the Psalmist brings all of that into view. God's word is a lamp to my feet, a light for my path. Because of that, then the one who chooses to follow God promises obedience to Him and His ways (v. 106)

--Even through suffering (v. 107)
--Even though life hangs in the balance (v. 109)
--Even through opposition (v. 110)

How is this possible, that someone will stay obedient in this situation? Well, once again the love of God's word is brought up to provide this answer. God's laws are my treasure. They are my heart's desire.

So, the big question for any believer -- is the law of God your actual desire...like how you desire a certain food, a certain good thing, a certain future hope, wishes for your children….is your desire like that?

Today, I urge you to take some time to get out some crayons or use colored pencils to draw out this idea of light and desire. That God's word is your desire and that it provides light to your path. I know you may think that you have no artistic talent, but as we know from our childhood…everyone can color with crayons. How "good" it is matters little. Just draw out your worship and your prayer to God; you can do it. He will think it is lovely. Then, once finished, hang it up somewhere as a reminder to you of both verses.

ס Samekh (Samech)

113 *I hate those with divided loyalties, but I love your instructions.*

114 *You are my refuge and my shield; your word is my source of hope.*

115 *Get out of my life, you evil-minded people, for I intend to obey the commands of my God.*

116 *LORD, sustain me as you promised, that I may live! Do not let my hope be crushed.*

117 *Sustain me, and I will be rescued; then I will meditate continually on your decrees.*

118 *But you have rejected all who stray from your decrees. They are only fooling themselves.*

119 *You skim off the wicked of the earth like scum; no wonder I love to obey your laws!*

120 *I tremble in fear of you; I stand in awe of your regulations.*

Let's think about movies again...think about a movie where a character has to be convinced about taking some course of action, to undertake some path or role or task that they obviously weren't going to before. One of my wife's favorite movies is the animated film *The Emperor's New Groove*. In that film, both of the main characters are forced to take a new course of action. The "good guy," voiced by John Goodman, has to be convinced to help the Emperor (now turned into a Llama) get back to his capital city. Pacha had just returned home from a long, and disappointing, trip to himself, and going out again simply wasn't in his plans. The Emperor, voiced by David Spade, has a different kind of new course of action in that at the start of the film, he is a selfish childish leader. Through the film, however, a new course of life into maturity where he truly takes on the aspect of caring for others as the leader of the nation emerges.

This section of the psalm provides an overview of life…that we each have a choice of path for our life. There is the path of the one who chooses to follow God's ways and there is the one who strays from God's decrees.

His warning to us is to not have divided loyalties between God and rejection of God. Clearly, as v.118 says, God rejects the ones who stray from His ways. My focus then is to love God's instructions. God and His instruction then become a refuge, a shield, and our source of hope (v. 114).

Often, in my own life, I feel the struggle in my mind. At times, events come in a way that make me sad, or to feel bad or upset. In that moment when I am struggling in the mind, I need to not get that divided mind, divided heart. What I really need is hope. I need a source of hope then to protect me. God then is that for me…I focus on Him and He is my source of hope. From there, with hope, I regain my strength because He is my refuge and shield.

With that confidence, I can speak clearly to the "evil minded." I demand the evil minded get out of my life. I refuse to let them influence to how I live. They want me to be double minded; I choose instead to be obedient to live well. What a great first step of confidence and clarity for how you live. Make the declaration: "I intend to obey the commands of my God."

What happens for me if I stay obedient:—God will sustain how I live, not let my hope be crushed, and He will rescue me. Because He sustains and rescues, I will meditate on law, on the Word. I will sink deeply His word into my mind.

If, though, I go to divided loyalties, and stray from God's decrees, a different, far worse thing will happen. Rather than having my life protected, He will take away life--"You skim off the wicked of the earth like scum." He will reject me and anyone who strays from His ways.

The wicked are fooling themselves, we are told. What do you think that means? I think it means that for many, they tell themselves that either there is no God (thus no future place of judgment) or that how they are living is good enough to avoid any negative future. They want to believe that regardless of what the Bible may suggest God wants, they are okay. God says, rather, that they are fooling themselves and that judgment will come.

So, in fear or awe of God, it is no wonder I obey. I tremble in fear. I stand in awe of His regulations. God does love all people and opens the door for all, but a person must respond. The Psalmist sees the greatness of God and recognizes that if a person rejects God, a path of destruction has been chosen. God will not sit idly by in the face of that….he will act in a way to "skim off the wicked of the earth." Based on our choices…don't have divided loyalty or be pulled in the direction of the evil-minded. Instead, say with the Psalmist, "I intend to obey the commands of my God."

Write out that phrase from verse 115. Again, post it around your life so that you can see it often. Post it on social media. Lock that thought into your mind.

ע Ayin

121 Don't leave me to the mercy of my enemies, for I have done what is just and right.

122 Please guarantee a blessing for me. Don't let the arrogant oppress me!

123 My eyes strain to see your rescue, to see the truth of your promise fulfilled.

124 I am your servant; deal with me in unfailing love, and teach me your decrees.

125 Give discernment to me, your servant; then I will understand your laws.

126 LORD, it is time for you to act, for these evil people have violated your instructions.

127 Truly, I love your commands more than gold, even the finest gold.

128 Each of your commandments is right. That is why I hate every false way.

This is the fourth section of the third division, focusing on what God's law provides. Here's what we have seen so far:

- 97-104: wisdom
- 105-112: life guidance
- 113-120: how to live in evil times

Today we see writing about "what to expect from God" or "what I want God to do for me." This section once again brings in the major themes, both the one about God's reaction to those who don't follow His ways and the theme of having a deep desire for God's laws.

The Psalmist shares eight things right out of the gate what he expects God to do.

1. Don't leave me at the mercy of my enemies (121)—we hear this in how Jesus taught us to pray, to ask God for protection from the evil one.
2. Guarantee me a blessing (122)—while perhaps bold, God urges us to ask Him for things, to seek Him, coming like a child expecting Him to provide.
3. Do not let the arrogant oppress me (122b)—we know the enemy will use others to bring us opposition; we know we aren't really battling against "flesh and blood," but against spiritual powers, and so standing in the full armor of God, we want to stand.
4. Let me see your rescue (123)—not just "rescue me," but let me see it. Often we need the tangible presence of God, just as Moses did when he asks to see God's face at the time of getting the 10 Commandments.
5. Let me see your promise fulfilled (123b)—in building of our hope, we want the evidence to carry us through; remembering the moments of God's prior promises help us stand in challenging times.
6. Deal with me in unfailing love (124)—acknowledging that I won't be perfect in all my actions, so that as we interact, don't execute the justice that You could, but rather work with me in love…and not just love, but love that is unfailing.
7. Teach me your decrees (124b)—more than once in the total Psalm, we make the statement of needing God to be our teacher, our professor helping us learn His rules for life.
8. Give me discernment (125)—link this back to v. 105 where we know that God's law is a lamp for my life, making my

way going forward. As we face a variety of circumstances, we need insight or discernment which we know comes from God.

Now, why should the speaker expect God to do these things? What can the speaker offer, or on what leverage?

"I am your servant"

Verses 124 and 125 are the clear admission of my place before God. I am not His equal. I am submitted to Him, making the claim that I am merely a slave to God. Paul writes to the Romans that we once were slaves to sin, but now are slaves to God (Romans 6:15-23)

There is a clear sense that the Psalmist is saying, "God, You owe me." I have given You my life, and places myself under your protection…so come through." Verse 126, restating how the section begins in v. 121, cries out for God act. Don't leave me to the mercy of my enemies.

The Psalmist closes with a blurting out an expression of joy. I think of Sam, the faithful servant in *The Lord of the Rings*, in his great love for Frodo, many times bursting out with tears of joy, of concern, when he sees his master in some situation. So, we come back again to this theme of "deep desire (with joy) for God's word, and in particular, the subtheme there of "loving God's word, ways, more than riches

"Truly I love your commands more than gold, even the finest gold."

That leads the Psalmist then to state what, to him, is obvious: Each command is right! That is why I hate every false way.

This expression of great joy throughout the psalm continues to blow me away as I study, and I pray it does for you as you study Psalm 119. This isn't just 176 verse of "obey God's commands or else." Instead, there is this constant refrain of how much the Christian should delight in God's ways. God's commands evoke my love, even more than gold…even more than the finest gold!!

Pray, God, we have no right to make claims on You, but You do invite us to bring our requests to Your throne. So, we do ask for You to be with us, to bless us, to show Your power in rescuing us and fulfilling Your promises. We do this because we are Your servant, and the actions of my life is one of joy, that I truly love your commands

פ Pe (Pey) (Peh) (Pei)

129 *Your laws are wonderful. No wonder I obey them!*

130 *The teaching of your word gives light, so even the simple can understand.*

131 *I pant with expectation, longing for your commands.*

132 *Come and show me your mercy, as you do for all who love your name.*

133 *Guide my steps by your word, so I will not be overcome by evil.*

134 *Ransom me from the oppression of evil people; then I can obey your commandments.*

135 *Look upon me with love; teach me your decrees.*

136 *Rivers of tears gush from my eyes because people disobey your instructions.*

The idea of law suggests always a question of obedience or not. The psalmist says quite confidently "I obey [Your laws]."

Why? Out of fear?

No…in keeping with the larger theme of "deep desire (with joy) for God's law," he states at the start in v. 129 "Your laws are wonderful." This of course hearkens back to his expression of joy and love from the previous section, in vv 127-128.

But then he keeps going explaining further about why someone should obey the law.

- First, harkening back to v 105 that the word, the laws are illuminating for how to walk, he says that the teaching of the law gives light (v. 130a)
- The law is not complicated, but rather easy to understand (v. 130b)
- The law and God's ways are like air, giving me breath, which the Psalmist says that he "pants with expectation." (v. 131a)
- Then, again with confidence, the law fulfills the longing of the one who follows God's way. (v. 131b)
- For the one who obeys, the law, God's way gives mercy. (v. 132)
- Then, looping back to v. 105, we are told that the law, God's word, will guide our steps. (v. 133)

If that is not enough, staying in obedience to God's way guides me so that I CAN avoid being overcome by evil. What a glorious thought…we obey and the word guides us. And how does it guide us, but walking in a way that I am not overcome by evil

The call to God for Him, if I follow it and obey, frees me from oppression of evil. Better, as Romans 6:16-23 discusses, we once were slaves to sin (see also John 8:34). We were held in captivity. We need saving. We need someone to ransom us.

The band MercyMe wrote a song called "Flawless" from their CD *Welcome to the New*. They sing "Then Like a hero who takes the stage when we're on the edge of our seats saying it's too late." Too late? We see the situation is fraught with danger; we can tell that a crisis is building and saving needs to happen. So, like in any great story, we look for the hero. Who is that hero who will ransom us?

Jesus!

In Matthew 20:28, Jesus says openly "for even the Son of Man came not to be served but to serve others, and to give his life as a ransom for many." Paul, years later writing to his own disciple Timothy said it this way: For there is one God and one mediator between God and mankind, the man Christ Jesus, who gave himself as a ransom for all people. (I Tim 2:5-6)

The Psalmist doesn't name Jesus…he doesn't know of Jesus…but he knows and believes what God has said that He will ransom us from evil.

Let's stop at verse 135. If God loves me, it is shown because He teaches me the decrees of life. The Psalmist calls to God for His love. "Look upon me with love" he asks…and by what evidence could God prove this? "Teach me your decrees."

We do need to obey the law. In the Mem section, we saw how we were given a recipe for success in vv 101-102: This provides a circle for life success (101-102):

--refused to walk on any evil path in order to remain obedient

--in being obedient "You have taught me well" so, I gain wisdom to know to NOT walk on any evil path

Here, we see another circle. God teaches me (v. 135) and that teaching gives light (v. 130); with that light I am guided and will not be overcome with evil. As I walk in the holy way, I call out to God for Him to look upon me with love, and prove that love through teaching me.

Pray, thanking God that His law provides obedience training for life.

צ Tsadhe (Tasdeh)

(136 Rivers of tears gush from my eyes because people disobey your instructions.)

137 O LORD, you are righteous, and your regulations are fair.

138 Your laws are perfect and completely trustworthy.

139 I am overwhelmed with indignation, for my enemies have disregarded your words.

140 Your promises have been thoroughly tested; that is why I love them so much.

141 I am insignificant and despised, but I don't forget your commandments.

142 Your justice is eternal, and your instructions are perfectly true.

143 As pressure and stress bear down on me, I find joy in your commands.

144 Your laws are always right; help me to understand them so I may live.

Tsadhe opens the last major division of the psalm. The psalmist spends these last five sections speaking about our need of rescue from God. There is a connection between this need for rescue and the theme of reacting against those who disregard God's law and/or ways.

Remember, the second large theme of the three secondary themes is opposition. But in 12 verses, the focus shifts from simply receiving opposition, but a response to that opposition and rejection of God's ways. This shouldn't surprise us. Since the poem indeed is a love poem about God's law, then it makes sense for the one in love to react when the object of love is rejected.

God (or His follower) reaction to those who disregard God's law or ways (12 references):

God rebukes or acts: 21, 78, 118, 119,
I react against them: 53, 113, 115, 128, 136, 139, 158, 163

This thrust of reaction is why we need to sneak back into the previous section, to see v. 136. "Rivers of tears gush from my eyes because people disobey your instructions." The reaction because of others ignoring God's ways, openly disobeying, is enough to bring rivers of tears. I wonder if the Psalmist is feeling Sadness? Maybe Anger? Perhaps Indignation? As we will see in a moment, I think that explosive emotion ("rivers of tears gush from my eyes") is because of the depth of feeling the disciple has for God's ways.

So, it is this merger of feeling persecuted, feeling the emotion of reacting (defending God, defending one's own choices) that flows into this last division of a cry for rescue.

Verse 141 could be a theme verse for the entire division. It is very important for this section. "I am insignificant and despised." Have you felt this way before? Many of us have; I certainly have. Verse 143 carries this feeling even more. You feel the pressure and the stress bearing down on you to the point that you may struggle to even get out of bed.

The psalmist calls us to a different perspective. Instead of giving up and wallowing in the insignificance feeling, we are called instead to focus on God. "I do not forget God's commands." Even more, rather than holding to the sadness of being attacked, "I find joy in God's commands." Yep, here it is again. When considering God's laws, they bring me delight. This is one of the nineteen references of the theme.

So, under the scrutiny of attack…three emotions or ideas come about God's commands:

--I am so emotional about it all, rivers of tears gush from my eyes because people reject God's commands.
--I do not forget God's commands.
--God's commands bring me joy.

Why is the psalmist so sure of these commands? Read the eight verses again. Underline these seven truths about God's commands in this section:

--fair v.137
--perfect v.138a
--trustworthy v.138b
--thoroughly tested v.140
--eternal v.142a
--perfectly true v.142b
--always right v.144

In his closing, the psalmist gives God a request. I hear it as plaintive, pleading. He is asking God to give him life. Help me stay alive, God. Rescue me. While the word "rescue" isn't used specifically in this section, it is correct to have this section leading into the last division of the Psalm. We need to be rescued.

How do I get to live? By knowing God's commands, His laws, His ways! Thus, the closing thought is that I acknowledge that I need God to teach me, to help me understand, so that I may live. I have to understand…yes…but what? The law. God's ways.

The commands give me life? No wonder my eyes gush with tears when people reject and disobey them. I love the law so much that I get emotional over those who don't follow your ways. I feel insignificant, I feel despised…I think I am going to break due to the pressure bearing down on me. But I am going to hold to God's law. I need God to give me life. How? That You, oh God, give me understanding of the law.

How do I have life? That You, oh God, give me understanding. Of what? Of the law. Father that is my plea. Your laws are always right. Help me understand them so that I may live. As I feel opposed, as I see people not following Your ways, as I feel cut off, unseen, attacked….I want to live. And that life only happens from You. You help me to live…and that rescue comes in as I gain understanding of your perfect, fair, tested and perfectly fair laws….that lamp to my feet, light to my path. This day help me see your hand in my life.

ק Qoph (Koph) (Qof)

145 I pray with all my heart; answer me, LORD! I will obey your decrees.

146 I cry out to you; rescue me, that I may obey your laws.

147 I rise early, before the sun is up; I cry out for help and put my hope in your words.

148 I stay awake through the night, thinking about your promise.

149 In your faithful love, O LORD, hear my cry; let me be revived by following your regulations.

150 Lawless people are coming to attack me; they live far from your instructions.

151 But you are near, O LORD, and all your commands are true.

152 I have known from my earliest days that your laws will last forever.

The Psalmist dives deeply into the request for rescue. His life is, from his perspective, is hanging by a thread. The consistent sense of attack has spilled out; lawless people are coming to attack me! God, come save me.

But, he doesn't start with the request first. Instead, he builds the case for why God should come. He lists four actions that are done consistently by him. This list would make a great starting point for any Christian wishing to grow in discipleship.

My actions to God:
- Pray with all my heart
- Cry out to God
- Rise early before the sun
- Stay awake through the night

Why, though, does he do these things? Why should you do these things? So God will hear me. Verse 145—answer me; verse 146—I cry out; verse 147—I cry out; verse 149—hear my cry.

What cry? My cry for rescue – lawless people are coming to attack me. I am already in need of being revived, meaning I am near death due to the constant pressure and attack. Now they are coming again, these people who live far from the very instructions that I love dearly.

In the end, the disciple must trust. How can we rely on Him?
--God is near
--God's commands are true
--God's ways have been known to me since my earliest days
--God's laws will last forever

That's a good place to stand and rest. The rescue will come.

Look back at the four actions the disciple takes before God: Pray with all your heart; cry out to God; rise early before the sun to be with God; let God be the last thought on your mind before you sleep at night. Today, work your way through this four-step list today. And tomorrow. And the next day…early in the morning, last thing at night, constant prayer, open cry to God.

ר Resh (Reish)

153 Look upon my suffering and rescue me, for I have not forgotten your instructions.

154 Argue my case; take my side! Protect my life as you promised.

155 The wicked are far from rescue, for they do not bother with your decrees.

156 LORD, how great is your mercy; let me be revived by following your regulations.

157 Many persecute and trouble me, yet I have not swerved from your laws.

158 Seeing these traitors makes me sick at heart, because they care nothing for your word.

159 See how I love your commandments, LORD. Give back my life because of your unfailing love.

160 The very essence of your words is truth; all your just regulations will stand forever.

This section of the psalm is a lament about suffering for God and being attacked. First line clearly names the point of the division: rescue me. The Psalmist really becomes direct with God here. He makes a list of demands, followed by another list of all the things He is doing for God. It's perhaps the closest He comes to being argumentative with God.

Previously, there have already been all the statements about being attacked, about his actions of faith to the laws of God and his deep love for God's ways. And of course this last division really emphasizes that need for rescue. But to this point, the psalmist has not let his frustration boil out, but it does here.

The demands to God:

- Look upon my suffering and rescue me (v. 153)
- Argue my case (v. 154a)
- Protect my life (v. 154b)
- Revive me by your regulations (v. 156)

He makes these demands because of doing these things for God:

- I have not forgotten your instructions (v. 153b)
- I have not swerved from your laws (v. 157b)
- I observe and judge traitors against You (v. 158)
- I love your commandments (v. 159a)

So, God, give me back my life!! By the point of verse 159b, the psalmist is almost mad. I don't know about you, but I resonate with this emotion so much. You live for God. You follow the rules. You look around and see so many, including those who claim to be Christians, NOT following God…and yet seeming to have great success. It's like he wrote back in the previous section, v. 150…lawless people living far from God's instruction. And yet, it can feel like God is not protecting you, not providing for you.

Of course, God IS there for you. And, as the totality of the Bible teaches, what we see in the world is not the full story. Not only is there an afterlife in which more of the story will emerge, both your own and these other people you observe, but even now in the present time you do not know exactly what God is or is not doing. As He warned Job, take care in what accusations you make against God.

The Psalmist knows this too. Thus, as the section closes, he expresses his trust in God.

I can trust God will take care of me because of these 5 reasons:
1. Because of how great His mercy is (v. 156)
2. Because of Your unfailing love (v. 159)
3. Because the essence of Your word is truth (v. 160a)
4. Because Your word is just and righteous (v. 160a)
5. Because Your regulations will stand forever (v. 160b)

Pray, God we hold to you, even when our need of rescue is highest…especially WHEN our need of rescue is highest. We have not swerved from Your laws. See how I love your commandments. And I know I can trust you…that you will indeed come to rescue me. The very essence of your words is truth. Thank you!

ש Shin

161 *Powerful people harass me without cause, but my heart trembles only at your word.*

162 *I rejoice in your word like one who discovers a great treasure.*

163 *I hate and abhor all falsehood, but I love your instructions.*

164 *I will praise you seven times a day because all your regulations are just.*

165 *Those who love your instructions have great peace and do not stumble.*

166 *I long for your rescue, LORD, so I have obeyed your commands.*

167 *I have obeyed your laws, for I love them very much.*

168 *Yes, I obey your commandments and laws because you know everything I do.*

This is the penultimate section of the psalm where the writer loops in all three of the subthemes: opposition to the one who follows God, the reaction by God (and the disciple) against those who disregard God's ways, and the disciple's joy, great desire, for God's laws and commands.

The idea of the emotion of love, what I have suggested to you is the entire point of the psalm (a love ode to God's law) explodes out of this section.

- My heart trembles ONLY at the Word
- I love your instructions
- Love of your instructions gives me peace
- I long for the Word
- I love your commandments very much

So, a summary section, or maybe a re-stating of the entire psalm emerges here in the Shin verses. Take a look:

- 161-62: opposition comes at me, but the Word is good, a great treasure....so I will keep after it. There is a hint of being eager to pursue it just like someone in pursuit of a hidden treasure.
- 163-164: God's regulations are just, so they are worth praise. Equally, they are worth my condemnation of false people, false actions. We may not like the idea of confronting or condemning others, but again we see this sense of being affronted at the rejection of something that we love deeply.
- 165: the law gives me peace and guidance and safe steps, just like we saw in v. 105, the great theme verse of the entire Psalm. Since I have this light, I won't stumble. Since I know I won't stumble due to my path being illuminated, I have great peace on the journey.
- 166-167: rescue desired—longing—and it is due to the disciple through a connection with obedience to the commands. Here again, though, not obedience out of duty, but rather obedience to the law that I love.
- 168: I CHOOSE to obey God's laws. This is vital, but I am aware that the obedience is wise that I do so since You know everything I do.

Walk faithfully with God. He will rescue in the challenges of life. Love His laws and His commands regardless of how much opposition it may bring. His ways are just, right, good, and worthy of praise in our lives. Fall more deeply in love with this law…let your heart tremble at His word. That way of life, His way of life, brings great peace and confidence in the journey.

Today, write out verse 165. As we have done several times during this study, this devotional guide for Psalm 105, place copies of the verse where you can see it. Post it on social media. While it is a declarative, the sentence also calls out an inquiry. Are you experiencing peace in your life? Do you feel as if you are stumbling through decisions? If so, then the verse asks the next harder question: do you love God's instructions? Remember, for God, sheer statement of affirmation is not enough…He expects to see actions tied to words of promise. Today, make it your plan to openly love His commands.

ת Taw (Tav)

169 *O LORD, listen to my cry; give me the discerning mind you promised.* ***170*** *Listen to my prayer; rescue me as you promised.*

171 *Let praise flow from my lips, for you have taught me your decrees.*

172 *Let my tongue sing about your word, for all your commands are right.*

173 *Give me a helping hand, for I have chosen to follow your commandments.*

174 *O LORD, I have longed for your rescue, and your instructions are my delight.*

175 *Let me live so I can praise you, and may your regulations help me.*

176 *I have wandered away like a lost sheep; come and find me, for I have not forgotten your commands.*

And now we arrive at the last of the 22 sections. The last section. Its been a powerful journey through the longest chapter in the Bible, the love ode to God's law in Psalm 119. We worked our way through four sections while hearing over and again three themes under the overarching concept of God's commands.

So, to end the psalm (and conclude the fourth division, the one about the need for rescue), the Psalmist provides a sort of "call and response" section.

The writing starts with a list of statements of "May God" and "Let Me"… With each one, the Psalmist then ties in a wish or request. Take a look:

Listen to my cry → give me discernment
Listen to my prayer→ rescue me as You promised
Praise flow from my lips→ because You have taught me
My tongue sings about the Word → because all the commands are right

What a beautiful pairing of ideas for the Christian. I will cry out to God, I will pray to him, looking for His insight for living and rescue. In response, praise and songs will come from my heart acknowledging that God has taught me, and what He has taught me is right.

The Psalmist isn't finished. In vv. 173-175 he expresses three specific requests:

- Give me help because I have chosen to follow Your commands
- Give me rescue (I long for it) because Your instructions are my delight
- Let me live (so I can praise You) because Your regulations help me

We've seen the idea of "let me live" again and again. In fact, I suppose I could have included as one of the subthemes (an idea that repeats itself through the text studied). Eleven times the Psalmist has confessed that God's law is somehow connected to my own life. You should go read them again: 17, 37, 40, 77, 92, 93, 107, 116, 144, 159, and here in verse 175.

Everyone I know wants to live, and wishes to live well. They certainly want to remain alive. They want a good life. Well, the Psalmist shares how, throughout the psalm, urging himself to live connected to God's law. By doing so, there is a sense of his writing then that God's owes life. Here in verse 175, the connection is by allowing me to live, I will spend my time in praise of God.

The section, and the entire Psalm, then has an interesting end. He admits that, "I have wandered away like a lost sheep." I am not fully sure if this means the Psalmist has declared to have sinned or simply an idea of not being focused on God's ways.

In any case, listen to the tenderness in his final request in the final verse: come find me. When my daughters were small, we would often play a simple version of "hide and seek." In those moments when the girls would go hide, even as they were trying to not be found...the greater joy that would elicit giggles and screams of joy came when I would find them. You see the same thing in a tiny baby when you play "peek-a-boo" with them. You are standing right there with them, but when their eyes get gently covered up only to quickly reveal that there you are...the one who loves them, what happens? The big smile. The look of joy.

God, come find me. As the Psalmist states, I too say openly that I still remember Your commands. I have made my decision to be devoted to You and Your ways. Now, even as I sometimes stumble or when I fail to act as You would hope, come and find me. I love You, and Your law. Come find me.

Conclusion

Take a look back at the first section, the first eight verses of Aleph. There is a link between the conclusion of the psalm and the start. I think that as God directed the Psalmist in writing, diligently working through the acrostic pattern, He planned for the psalm to become something of a circle of unity.

In the first verses, the Psalmist speaks of following, of searching for God. Of wanting to walk in His paths. Then in verse eight, he ends the section by stating, "don't give up on me." At the end of the psalm, verse 176 presents this same idea: "come and find me" even as I may have wandered away.

Back at the start, we are shown the exact same reason for why God should stick with me: I will live holy.

What is it to live holy?
- v. 4—keep the commands carefully
- v. 5—actions consistently reflect His decrees
- v. 6—not ashamed at my life choices that match commands
- v. 7—consistently living as I should learning His righteous regulations
- v. 8—I will obey His decrees

My life will reflect His commands, the same commands that in verse 176, I promise that I have not forgotten.

You and I both want life. We want a life that is good, pleasing and not full of error. God has a way for us to get there. It comes by following His ways. Again and again, in Psalm 119 and elsewhere in the Bible, God desperately points us to the way of life. He illuminates the path, promising to give us insight as to the choices we should make. To have this good life, He calls us to follow His commands. He begs us to trust Him.

The Psalmist says again and again, the law is my delight. The commands are more valuable to me than riches. I pray that you can join him in that statement of declaration.

These commands are good. They are my delight.

They are a lamp for my feet, a light on my path.

I love them.

"Carl Creasman will bring a word and story to students that will ring with authenticity . . .and plant seeds of transformation in their thinking.
Ken Dillard, University of Cincinnati, Campus Pastor Collegiate Ministry

"Carl Creasman is an innovative speaker. Students relate well to the ideas, presentation, and realization of all that Carl offers."
Amy Boyer, College of Holy Cross

"Your presentation on 'Extreme Living Extreme Valor' drove home a message that was critical to the times we are living in. As you spoke to the audience about integrity, honor, & honesty, you could feel the emotion in the crowd as they took it in."
Michael Cowles, SkillsUSA Ohio Director

"Your words were inspirational, humorous and timely."
Dr. James T. King, Vice Chancellor Tennessee Board of Regents

"Carl has been instrumental in discipling me and challenging me….He will not back down from a challenge to his faith and is open and up-front about what Christ did for him."
Rev. Kyle Gatlin, Covenant United Methodist Church, Dothan, AL

"You have a special talent to inspire, motivate and excite others toward being the very best they can be."
Dr. Kermit Carter, Dean for Student Affairs, Calhoun Community College, Decatur, AL

"Carl has a unique way to speak the truth in a way that communicates to a 21st century audience."
E. Bailey Marks, Campus Crusade for Christ, Leader-Led Movements

"Carl's ability to relate to students and professionals alike makes his work extremely relevant to both audiences."
Victor Felts, South-Eastern IFC Executive Director

"Carl's passion for God and zeal for life continue to inspire me. His trust in God in all circumstances is a continual reminder to me of God's faithfulness."
Scott Allen, Former National Collegiate Ministry, Belmont College

To invite Carl to speak at your school, conference, or church, contact:
Carl E. Creasman, Jr.
P.O. Box 2031
Winter Park, FL 32790-2031
321.245.6882 or creasman@mac.com
www.carlcreasman.com

www.ingramcontent.com/pod-product-compliance
Lightning Source LLC
Chambersburg PA
CBHW031416040426
42444CB00005B/586